Lemmy Kilmister
Motörhead:
Color the Ace of Spades

FERAL HOUSE
ADULT COLORING BOOKS

Lemmy Kilmister of Motörhead
Color the Ace of Spades
© 2016 Feral House

· ·

The publisher wishes to thank
Christina Ward, Monica Rochester and
Elizabeth Perikli for their assistance.
Design by D. Collins

· ·

Feral House
1240 W. Sims Way Suite 124
Port Townsend, WA 98368

· ·

www.FeralHouse.com

TITLE: *Lemmybird* | ARTIST: *Allison Westbrook*

ARTISTS' STATEMENT: *I'm an illustrator that uses various media, but works mostly digitally these days. Though my personal work is usually sci-fi or fantasy based I find fun in drawing/painting just about anything. Doing this drawing of Lemmy was fun because I got to use an app (Procreate) on my iPad to do the initial sketch. The "inking" was done in Photoshop and I think the final piece turned out well, showcasing Lemmy's legendary "not having it" personality.*

ARTIST: *Dennis Franklin*

ARTISTS' STATEMENT: *I created an illustration in honor of Lemmy playing one of hie early gigs with Hawkwind on February 13th 1972 at The Roadhouse. The band played a benefit show for The Greasy Truckers. The show was recorded live and the original vinyl release is a coveted original vinyl release is a coveted Hawkwind record. I decided to do a Hawkwind record. I decided to do an illustration honoring this monumental event.*

TITLE: *Love & Light* | ARTIST: *Mica O'Herlihy*

TITLE: *Lemmy* | ARTIST: *Jim Blanchard*

ARTIST: *Dan Thomas*

ARTIST: *Rick Klu*

TITLE: *Lemmy in Nuthuggers* | ARTIST: *James Zolo*

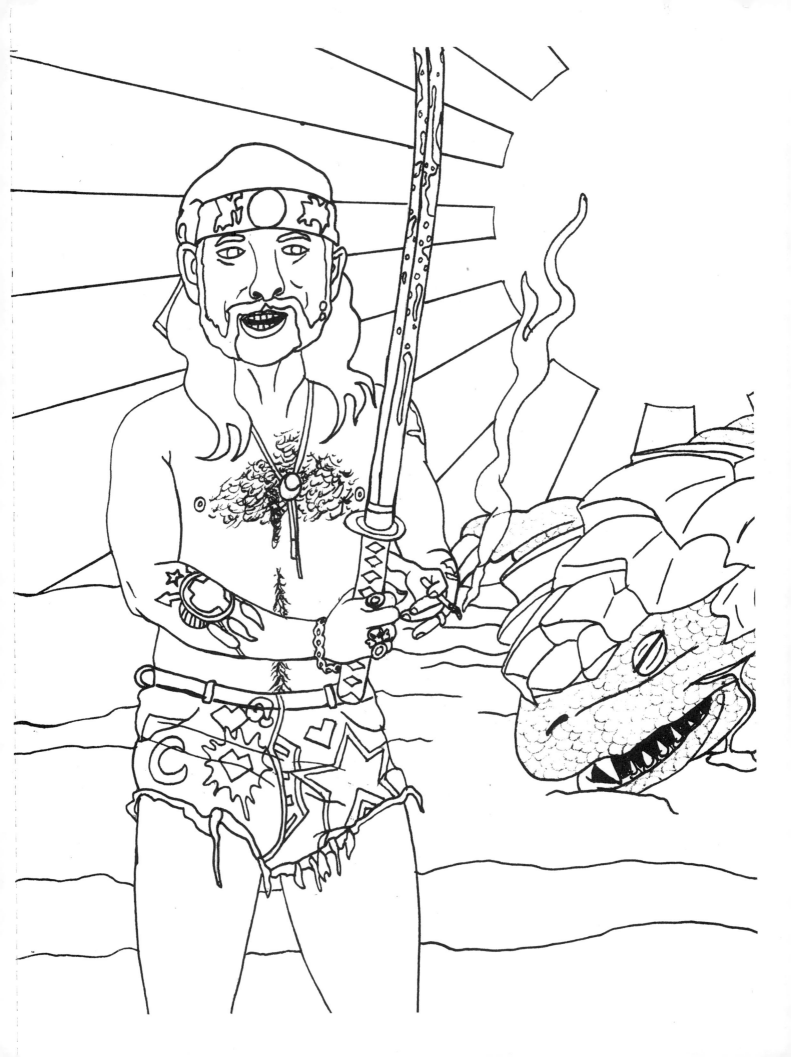

ARTIST: *Brytanni Burtner*

TITLE: *Lemmy Motormouth* | ARTIST: *Tony Millionaire*

ARTIST: *Mike Diana*

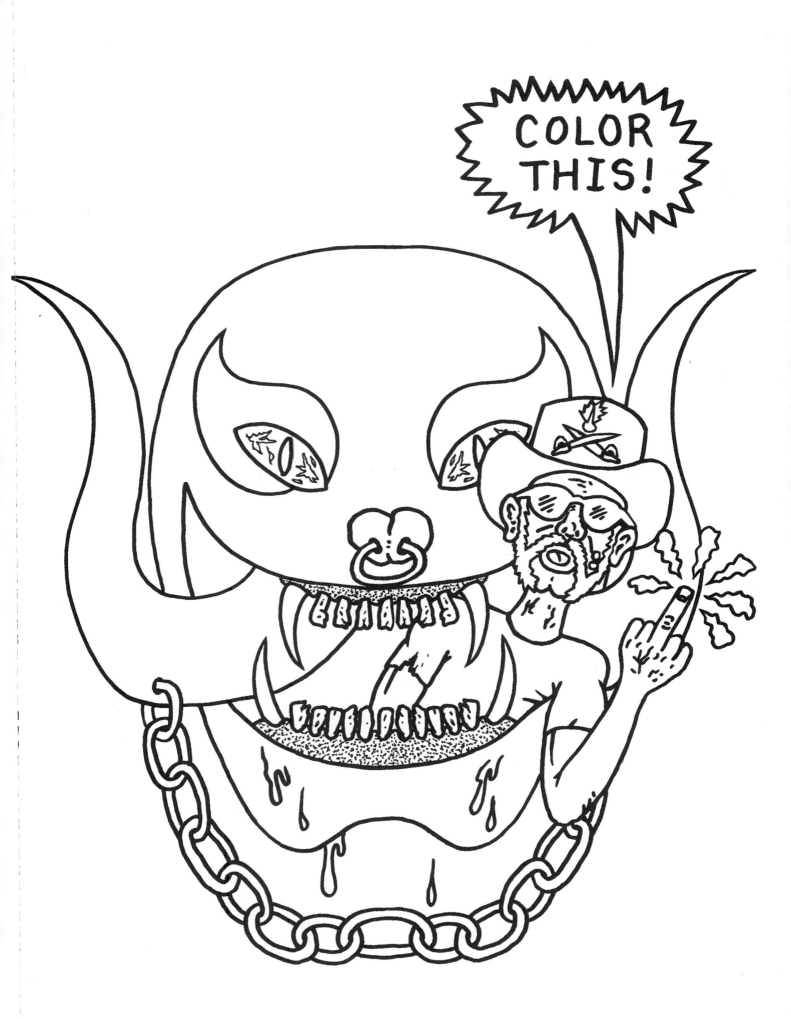

TITLE: *Ace of Spades Tarmac Man* | ARTIST: *Jon Tarry*

ARTISTS' STATEMENT: *Lemmy, Ace of Travellers, a section of the most frequented of many airports runways Lemmy took off and landed at. Lemmy Ace of Spades Tarmac Man*

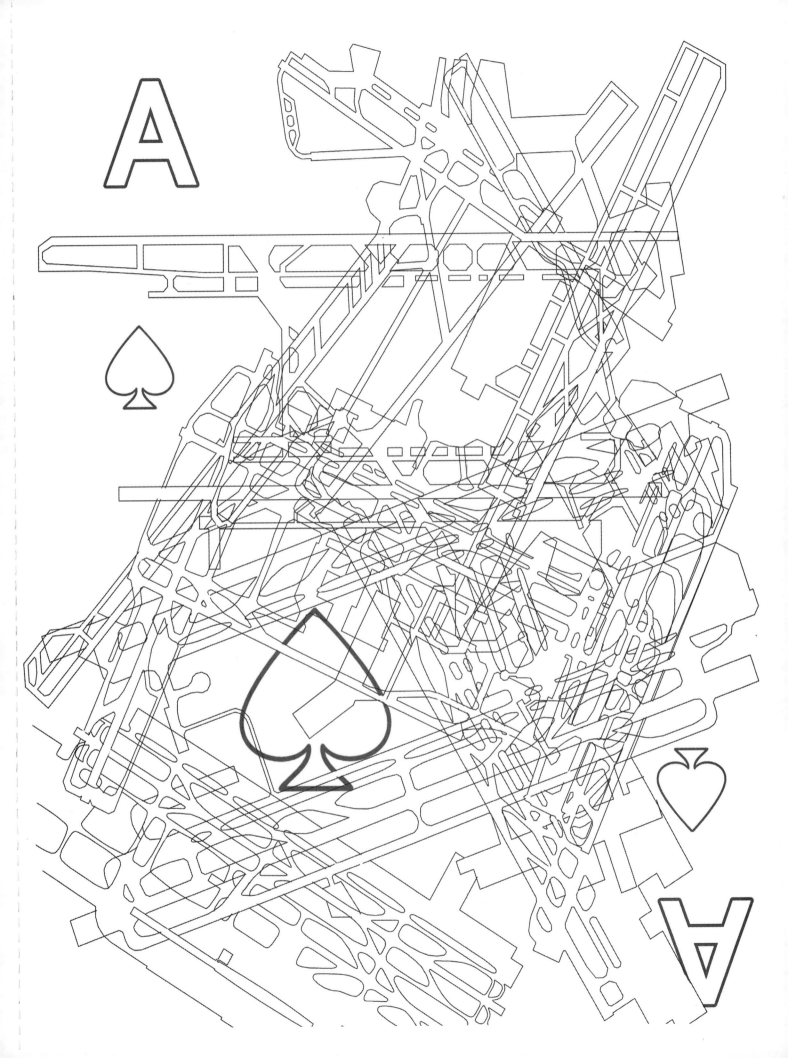

TITLE: *Lemmy's Army* | ARTIST: *Aiden Cook*

ARTISTS' STATEMENT: *Lemmy from Motorhead leads his army through the wasteland as a nuclear bomb detonates*

ARTIST: *Brytanni Burtner*

14

ARTIST: *Steven Abrams*

15

TITLE: *Eat My Beer Can* | ARTIST: *Jeffrey Maris*

.MY EATING BEER CAN — JEFFREY MARIS 2016

ARTIST: *Dan Thomas*

ARTISTS' STATEMENT: *Ian "Lemmy" Kilmister. His band Motorhead was the musical guest in a 1984 episode of the raucous BBC comedy "The Young Ones".*

TITLE: *Lemmy is God* | ARTIST: *Jason Atomic*

ARTISTS' STATEMENT: *As a teenage headbanger back in the NWOBHM days of the 80ies I would often see "LEMMY IS GOD" scrawled on the backs of studded and patched up denim 'battle jackets'. The irony of a confirmed atheist being deified by his fans was not lost on me. Once I coupled that with the fact that, the Capricornian, Lemmy shared his birthday with the mythical anniversary of Jesus the idea of this heavy metal crucifixion seemed a logical step.*

TITLE: *Lemlaut* | ARTIST: *David Durrett*

ARTISTS' STATEMENT: *My submission is a portrait of Lemmy Kilmister with the signature moles on his face forming the notorious umlaut that was gratuitously applied to the second "o" in the Motörhead logotype. I call it "Lemlaut."*

TITLE: *Moto* | ARTIST: *Mica O'Herlihy*

ARTIST: *Steve Krakow*

ARTIST: *Jimmy Dimmick*

TITLE: *Lemmy Playing* | ARTIST: *James Zolo*

TITLE: *Hell Bike* | ARTIST: *Uranus*

TITLE: *The Finger* | ARTIST: *Elliot Feldman*

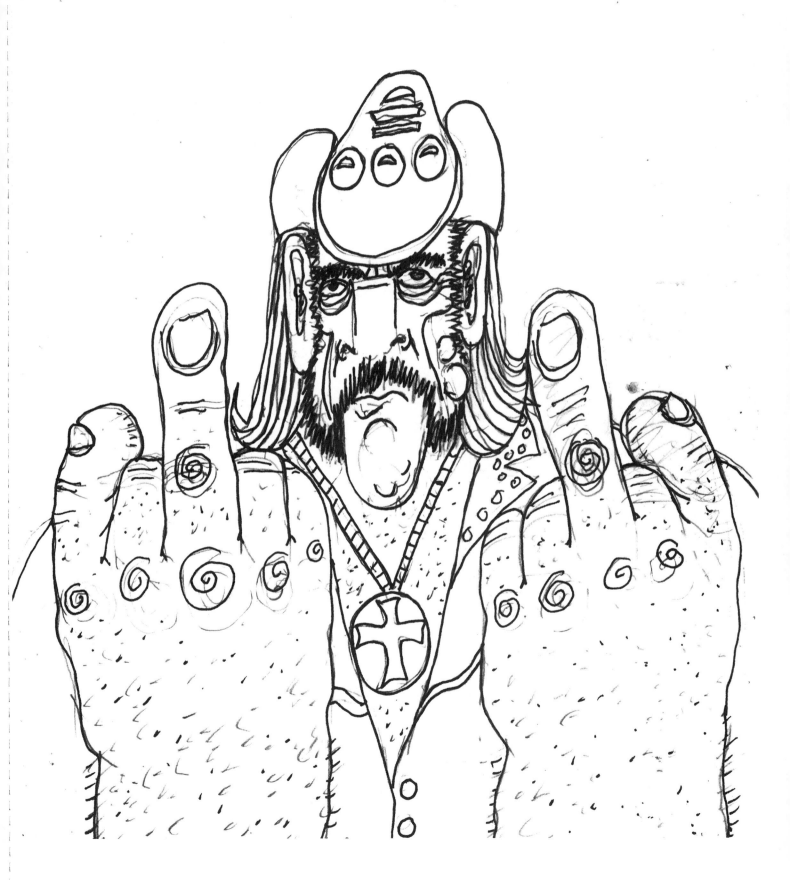

TITLE: *Lemmy in Hell* | ARTIST: *James Zolo*

ARTIST: *Carlos Apablaza Baschmann*

TITLE: *Lemmy's Kidz* | ARTIST: *Charles Krafft*

THE ADVENTURES OF THE KILMISTER KIDZ

LEMMY'S MOLES —
(GERBLES & GARY)

Charles Krafft '16

ARTIST: *Dan Wieken*

ARTIST: *Dawn Aquarius*

TITLE: *Chesty* | ARTIST: *Mica O'Herlihy*

ARTIST: *David Durrett*

ARTIST: *Chris Tischler*

ARTISTS' STATEMENT: *As an artist, I usually create abstract works, so making an actual drawing of someone came as somewhat of a challenge for this book. However, if you're doing a likeness of the great Lemmy, it might as well look like something a 14-year-old would draw on the back of his notebook in school. So in that case, job done.*

TITLE: *Murder One* | ARTIST: *Mica O'Herlihy*

TITLE: *Lemmy & Wendy* | ARTIST: *Michelle Witchipoo*

ARTIST: *Corinne Halbert*

TITLE: *Jack and Lemmy* | ARTIST: *James Zolo*

TITLE: *Eyeballz* | ARTIST: *Mica O'Herlihy*

ALI

Feral House is proud to collaborate with writer Darius James on the next editions in the Feral House Coloring Book Series (Muhammad Ali and Prince). James is the author of the classics That's Blaxploitation: Roots of the Baadasssss 'Tude (Rated X by an All-Whyte Jury) and Negrophobia: An Urban Parable.

"Just as he was for many Americans, Muhammad Ali's appearance on the cultural landscape was a turning point in my life. The moment he proclaimed I am the greatest, more so than Stokely Carmichael's call for Black Power! or Jamil Abdullah Al-Amin (H. Rap Brown) utterance Burn, baby, burn!, he demonstrated it was possible to speak truth to power. This is a quality Ali reflected throughout his life. Speaking truth to power.

PRINCE

Publisher, Adam Parfrey said of James, "Darius is the perfect person to curate this collection of art and prose created in honor of Ali and Prince." Feral House Coloring Books have quickly generated buzz in the book industry with their underground commix sensibility and mix of established and outsider artists. Each volume quickly sells out as a wholly collectible object d'art, not just a coloring book.

But on coloring books? Prince says it best:
In this life
You're on your own
And if de-elevator tries to bring you down
Go crazy!

With crayons. Through his music, Prince inspired unrestrained joy. With contributions from both Prince's fan-art community and professional illustrators, the Prince coloring book will be a pure expression and celebration of the joy he inspired throughout the world."

FERAL HOUSE
ADULT COLORING BOOKS